NEW WORD ORDER

The Poetry Of Otep Shamaya

Centaurs Breed Publishing

NEW WORD ORDER

The Poetry Of Otep Shamaya

All words & images Copyright © OTEP SHAMAYA 2011

Centaurs Breed Publishing

For information about this publication contact:
you@artsaves.me or online at www.otepsaves.me

Cover design & additional illustrative contribution
by Joey James www.joeyjamesart.com

This is a work of fiction. Names, characters, places, and incidents, either are the product of the author's imagination or are used fictitiously. And any resemblance to actual persons, living or dead, business establishments, events, or locales is entirely coincidental.

All rights reserved. No part of this publication may be reproduced or transmitted in any form or by any means, electronic, or mechanical, including photocopy, recording, or any information storage and retrieval system now known or invented, without permission in writing from the publisher.

"To me, the greatest pleasure of writing is not what it's about, but the music the words make." — Truman Capote

4

Dedicated to my friends that listened, that stayed true, and my loved ones who believe, endlessly. Thank you for answering at 4AM, for helping me move the mind furniture, for hearing me out, for standing beside me in the fire.

o   t   e   p

Table of Contents

11. Giant Prayers
14. Feeding My Muse
15. This Is Why
20. WMN
21. Bag Of Bones
23. Crawling Up
27. Gadfly
34. Nine Eleven
35. USA MA
41. Writing
44. Pardon Me
47. Painted On The Wall
49. The First Time
52. Single File
54. You Call
59. Baby Gods
62. Roma
64. Populi
67. Blood Of Caesar
69. At The Fountain
71. Roman Noon
74. Piazza de Renzi
76. Cheap Wine

81. Ringworm
85. Slow Night
90. Connection
93. Mid Night Mare
95. Rodent King
101. EX O
103. Wet Lung
109. The Whole Thing
110. Occupy Everywhere
112. A Bee
116. Compassionate Entomology
118. Bats & Hats
121. Widow at the Window
127. Miss
128. Cavity
132. Charlatan
136. Pussy
138. Bloodsucker
139. Look
141. Above All
144. On The Wall
145. To Begin
146. Flame Thrower
148. For Love
153. Big Red

157. One Truth
158. Spiritual Intercourse
162. Notice To The Human Race
164. Feminine Force
168. Def Poetry
173. Loving Home
176. Founder Of The Feast
177. Somebody Please
178. Grave Words
182. Ithaca
183. Don't Go
186. Sadistic Scribbles

GIANT PRAYERS

breathing
in   the
      fire
volcanic
ash-
swollen
lungs
thick
as fresh honeycomb
buzzing
like a red hive
within
the wild winds
of a lost world
pressing the firm earth
with quiet feet
tough enough
to run
inside the sun
cracked clay
like broken
dinner plates

footprints
in rich
coffee
colored
soil
leading
everywhere
in one direction
    a girl
looking to
a woman
looking to
a world
with broken eyes
shades and radiances
of dreams that faded
of dreams that caked
into reality
the weight
the vacancy
chains of vapor
tranquility
of salvation
on hiatus

NEW WORD ORDER

the virus of language
pages and pages
of giant prayers
from a tiny heart
shriveled
& gilded
from
the mass
murderous
burden
of cold
cavernous
love
lost
in
the
spiraling
conspiring
dark.

FEEDING MY MUSE

And into my ear,
breath fluttering
like a butterfly,
  her words came
  as she did,
"my God",
her thighs
tightened
and drew me in,
"MY GOD"

  & my reply,
  a penetrating
  kiss
  a bite
  on the lip
  & a breathless
  selfish,
"yes?"

THIS IS WHY

we occupy
because our country
is broken
because we care enough
to (at least) try to
(at least) shine a light on
or (at least) try to
fix it

    this is why
    we occupy

because we believe ALL are created equal

because they continue to perpetuate and legislate inequality among the races, sexes, orientations, creeds, & beliefs

because they want to silence free speech and diminish our civil liberties

because we believe in the Bill of Rights

because we don't believe anything supercedes The Constitution

> this is why
> we occupy

because our government pursues economic policies that only benefit the rich

because we believe in separation of corporation and state

because the average CEO's salary exceeds the amount their corporation pays in income taxes

because 49% of Americans live below or behind the poverty line - that's almost 150 million Americans which is more than the population of The United Kingdom, France, Greece, & Switzerland combined

because they continue to cut welfare for hungry people but pour billions more into corporate welfare using our tax dollars

       this is why
       we occupy

because we want decent jobs, economic opportunities, & affordable healthcare

because they want to destroy the working class and create a new caste system of dependent peasants

because our air is toxic and our water is foul

because they rail against nationalized healthcare while using nationalized healthcare to help their families and loved ones stay healthy

because we are impatient, because we are sick of waiting for the corrupt to fix themselves, we may be clumsy but (at least) we're trying

       this is why
       we occupy

because they send brave men & women of the armed forces to fight unnecessary wars

because 59% (550 Billion Dollars) of our National Budget is spent on the Defense Department while 2% is spent on Justice, Agriculture, & Energy, and 6% on Education & Health, and the rest dissipates in bureaucracy

because most of us are patriots, parents, students, veterans, we are the heart and hands of this nation

>　this is why
>　we occupy

because the average income of the top 1 percent has gone up by more than 250 percent

because the incomes of "average" Americans have fallen by 6 percent

because they fight to protect high-end tax breaks for the wealthiest Americans, and do nothing to prevent tax increases for 160 million "average" Americans because they use religion to excuse their cruelty

because they cherry pick the gospels to suit their devilry (Matthew 19:24)

because the banks can rob the world and it's legal, but a hungry man robs a bank and he's a felon

because they claim to love the free market but fight to support monopolies

>   this is why
>   we occupy

because we, the people, didn't get a bail out

because they blame our generation for the failures of this nation when they're the ones who raised us

because though we know it's inconvenient, we are trying to change
the   world.

WMN

a lullaby
ghosts over
the quiet room

      they cracked the crown
      to pluck the pearl
      here,
      on the jagged edge
      of the world

set to the drama
of mama
in the backroom
drunk again
daddy
with the servants
committing sin
brother
fighting back
a devilish grin
& daughter's chasing snakes
    with a paper and pen.

BAG OF BONES

leaving a crater
in the sheets
    lathered
in the aftermath
heaving hearts
    beat
to the top
of trembling skin
pink petals
wet with a kiss
    set adrift
on a blanket sea
I & she
one life stand
    for the
        moment
of lust
and trust
closer than
any humans
can be
in the coil

        captured
in the breath
and air
we share
        fingers braided
        lungs ablaze
bag of bones
bag of bones
        heavy
        as river stones
milky limbs
interwoven
scattered
across the
tangles of
a dreaming
blanket   maze.

CRAWLING UP

from the wreckage
daily
    a life of
crawling up
    from the crater
    from the dent
    from the depths
    from the flames
    from the edge
    from the bottom
    from the awful
    emptiness
crawling up
    my spine
    into my mind
crawling up
    from the grave
    from the waves
    from the bane
    of sadness
    surrounding me
    drowning me

crawling up
    daily
    unwavering
    away
    to escape
    from the pain
    from the way
    that they
        break
        me
        down
crawling up
    for the light
    for the fight
    for the slight
    pinhole
    diamond
    shining
    through
    the lazy hues
    of the vast
    expanse
    of the endless night
crawling up

        over the lip
        down the dune
        through the ruins
        from the dust
        and savage sand
        to the next
        craggy
        shaft
        of soggy loam
                slipping back
        down the sludge
        gripping with
        fists
        coated
        in stinking mud
crawling up
        digging in
spirit split
splintered needles
chipped and thin

a pause
to reclaim my breath
to punish these dreams

      of quiet surrender
      to remember
            that I do NOT stop
                  I don't give up
                  I don't give a fuck
                  I don't give in
                  so I begin
            again
      crawling up
      crawling out
      crawling away
            over the moaning
            bones
            of those
            who chose
            to quit
      &   remain.

GADFLY

ignore
at your
own peril
one nation
divided
incited
ignored
& bored
tax the poor
reward the rich
ignore the gospel
Wall Street apostles
scuttle the vaults
abolish government
cut syntax
      praise sin tax
raise
creationist
      music
of crisp
sound bites
to quiet

the lazy
crazy
cries
& pleas
for jobs
PLEASE
  by nut jobs
  con jobs
jerk offs
work off
the pounds
petition jockeys
ferocious electorate
press
the flesh
ignore the rest
  believer & deceiver
self-caliphate
genuinely
  impotent
generally
  insolvent
gravely
  important

disciplined
to betray
    out of context
    here on earth
under god
king makers
holy war
holy whore
starve
the peasants
or eat the rich
silk suited jesters
pretending to be Caesar
    feverish lips
dripping with spit
    summoning
the pitchfork hordes
to rise up
against
    their own
against
    their home
to protect
the greasy

necks
of these
diseased
> freaks &
> phonies
> frauds &
> marauding
> zombies

of Wall Street
feasting on
American meat
marrow & bone
> to each his own

ignore us doing this
ignore us doing this
> robbing you blind

guns god gays
taxes & terrorists
propaganda & prayer
propaganda & prayer
> silence

as the
flags ripple
in the toxic air

   it's a myth
the bias
of science
the forest
  is a lie
the streams
  are early mud
the sky
  is mined
& so is the shore
it's ours
  not yours
but you can see
for a fee
the sludge
that once was
the clear blue sea
crowded now
with death
& bloated bone
smokestacks
& acid baths
& nuclear powered
satellite towers

      for you
to connect
your wealth
with your status
symbols
      just continue to
      ignore us doing this

roads paved
with graves
praise
or peril
tame
& sterile
        oh get off
        the cross
    tiny
    blue
    dot
in an inky
sea
    alone
godless
lawless

with but
love to
keep us
warm
and guide us home
      time to
turn off
tune in
we ignore the song
but know the tune
gnawing   at   our   bones.

Nine Eleven

Today, I will create.
I will let joy carbonate my blood.

      I will inhale life.
      I will inhabit this very moment.
      I will remember.
      I will reflect but
I   will   push   on.

USA MA

see sick
shot
in the dark
in the ocular cavity
dual missiles
fired into
the towering
skyscraper
of a man
made of
ego
& filth
      shattered
      glass
gunpowder
burning
through
the drapes
of tissue
breaking
the chassis
of

your damaged
body
    crumpled
like the twisted steel
of ground zero
fractured bone
and ribbons of meat
    fear
spearing
your heart
in the violence
of the lonely,
lonely
    dark
eyes
that once
cloaked
the world
with hate
    blinded
by the razors
of arrogance
    now
    punched

in
and bloodied
pink meat
and scorched
bone
eyes
that once
saw visions
of the Prophet
that once saw millions
in post-war apocalyptic
    profit
that swallowed
the camera
that bugled
your message
eyes
that once hypnotized
    now thicken
    into
    beefy oysters
rotting
and stained
    the last image

        burned
        onto the
        mirror
        of your lens
        is the flash
        of an American
        made death
        machine
created in your
honor
        empty
        eyes
staring
out
as they
wrapped
you
in plastic
        stars and stripes
waving over the
rubble of you
and the
crusted
black

punctures
where your
eyes once were
    now
      witness
      nothing
sunk at sea
the dragon
      anchored
in the deep
food for hagfish
sucking skin
brittle bone
to coral reef
lost in the
    echo
of Babylon
ashes to splashes
dust to rust
we say
with all
due disdain,
    "fuck you,
      you died a coward"

. and we cheered
and we danced
and welcomed amnesia
for the death of a devil
      "fuck you, footnote.
fuck   you,   forever."

WRITING

words, surging like sunbeams
through the window shade,
nourish my naked soul
contours
and blight
pinned
to the walls
    by my
    light
dead
days
& memories
pollinate
the gold split
half moon
crescent
smile
in spite
of my
life's
soft
bisected

journey
forward
and onward
bigger and better
greater things
than these
      pygmy giants
casting monstrous
shadows
to break
      the climb
to stall
      the ascent
but my
fists
are gripped
and ready
words
will save me
believe this
now
      . words
      . will
      . save

my fire is bright
my soul is brave
so
troubled seas
or exotic coast
the helm
is mine
where I go
is up to me
the wind
will gust
but it won't
disrupt
I shall simply
shift my sails
and   suck   it   up.

PARDON ME

I don't mean
to disappoint
but I'm celestial
    not a rock star
I shine and burn
but only to
evolve and learn
to bring light
to the darkness
of this life
I'm inked and
punctured
but my glyphs
are not for you
visual vultures
to pick apart
and discard
these are my
journeys
my lost loves
my silent prayers
my tribal

devotions
        my holy scars
I don't do drugs
but I am addictive
word lust junkie
art & women
knowledge
of the pagan night
purple halo
radiating from my soul
stretching wings
to extend my flight
what you see
may not be
what I am
        I am marked
like a leopard
like a prisoner
like a bumblebee
like a lightning strike
rare in form
and frightening
to most
but when my shell

is set to soil and I have bid thee farewell I want my flesh to a be a map of my journey and show the worms how well I did excavating joy from a heartless world so full of cruelty that it's hard to see beauty even when it's right in front of you, even when it's me.

PAINTED ON THE WALL

America is not at war.

The United States Armed Forces are at war.

    America is at the mall.

a tented mob outside of a retail store is greeted with applause

a tented mob non-violently supporting social justice is greeted with pepper spray and iron bars

and they say
this is Capitalism

they say this
is Democracy

I say, this is why we Occupy
I say, come on lover

spread those lips

raise your fist
and   FIGHT.

THE FIRST TIME

the instant,
orbits collide
trading breath
in the liquid
of our stare
the séance of seduction
hunger and fear
skin meets flesh
the power of a kiss
      dark and deep
the infinite moment
      of crushing bliss
earth trembles
and heaven quakes
blood boils
at the taste of strength
eyes flare
with heated stares
falling to
a bed of fire
tongues
touching

in the surge,
in the break
lips join
and hover
then crush
and cover
like savages
in winter famine
like pagans
howling
beneath the moon
    feeding
    the beast in me
    mouth wet
    with the depth of you
her back arches
and lace releases
down the smooth
poles where her
ankles meet
she opens
like a lotus flower
and I suckle the
sweet honey of her sex

and for a moment
there is only us
no rent to pay
no bills to see
no children starving on TV
      just the silk of her skin
      merged with mine
      the rhythm of our bodies
      existing outside of time
selfish, but giving
selfless, but existing
to reach the thrust
of thunder
together
to taste the wonder
of forever
in a symphonious crescendo
that will be soaked
in a drunken dream
to merry memories
of a night well spent
with a lover I just met
in   a   ·golden   eternity.

SINGLE FILE

nothing's new
it's all the same
every day
    eat to erase
    boredom
    television
    thinks for me
    sex with friends
    the gym again
    wholly unholy
    but
    anchors away
    not today
    silence
    is the only
    voice I hear
    I check the mirror
    just so
    I can see
    a living face
no poetry
eats me

no love
has seized my heart
      my only hope
      is career
      my only wealth
      is art
      my only salvation
      is at the end
      of this
sentence.

YOU CALL

    & your words
freeze the blood
in my veins
    your distance
swells the friction
between us
my heart wants
    to scream
but chokes
    on silence
I want to tell you
the many ways
I love you
the many ways
we work
how
    our love
fortifies me
but
the black hole
of your soul
devours

everything
you
you
you
you are overwhelmed
you are too busy
you have nothing
you are unavailable
you feel sad
you feel betrayed
you feel trapped
you are lonely
you are bored
you are uninspired
you are celebrating
nothing
ever again
and everything I've said
has just made it worse
so
instead
we discuss the weather
and the dismal day
and the simple way

everyone
& everything
agitates you
and I feel so small
and sucked in
and retching
on the relics
of what lived in the haze
the idea of us
the hope & prophecy
that lingered in your eyes
  the flame
  the flicker
that licked up & burned
the mundane away
  and I panic
  and I stop
  and listen
for hours
  to the bullets
  & bullshit
fired from your empty heart
  and I inhale
  a breath so deep

        it could dry the sea
        and your sickness
        becomes mine
        and I decide not to flee
        and I embrace
what's left
this carcass
of what
was once
    we
and I act tough
and I feign brave
and draw back
the tears
and
secretly
whisper
how much
I miss
    the myth
    the fable
    the tale
    the phantoms
there were once

you   &   me.

BABY GODS

dreaming
in the warmth
of each other
my darlings,
      you are the
atoms of my soul
crawling
and clawing
through the
      loam
to heal me
with the ink
of your eyes
drawing
me in
to rewrite
the life
      we share
I, slave
you, master
      baby gods
architects

of time
knitting
the armor
around my heart
without
    you
I am hollow
so I hold you
close & pray
for this holy
moment to
forever stay
    in me
      with me
    my hope
for perfect love
returned
with a kiss
a wag
and a yip
    no strings
      attached
no conditions
or concessions

I hold tight
and never
ever
want to let you go.

ROMA

stepping
on stones
of time
crags and valleys
watercolor sky
temper
the ruins
      with odes
      and omens
of the Imperialist mind
priests and peasants
kings and captives
gold on the names
of the forgotten
riches and recipes
rotted to dust
pillars of nothing
      phantom empire
speak only lies
of the realm
that was
gardens of rock

screaming
  for a soul
  for a heartbeat
  for heartache
for anything
just another chance
to taste the rain
to touch the air
to hear the people
to be aware
of how grand it is
to be
to be
to   be.

POPULI

    most of you are forgettable
        and you know it
    but if you're lucky
        and we're not
    something about you
        will remain
        will stain
        the memory
        bank
    maybe the shoes
    those stinky sneakers with tattered laces
    or the leather flats with green stitching
    perhaps it's the blue wool vest
    or the knitted shawl
        or the way you made fun of the one
        who just gave their all
    maybe it's the cologne you wear (too much of)
    or the sports car keychain conspicuously dangling from your golden woven knitted jean pocket
        or maybe it's the way
        you called her a bitch because

        she   didn't   acknowledge   your   swollen wallet
maybe it's
        the red wristwatch
        the black leather bag
        the hardened hair glazed in gel
        the silver pinky ring
        the ripped tights
or the freak you just put through hell
        maybe
        it's
the way you pushed past
the emptiness in your laugh
so no one will see
that
all these things
every plastic
piece
everything you seem to be
        is a lie
you are forgettable
and you know it
so you try
to disguise
the empty

bowl
within your soul
with things
that distract
and detract
from the
translucent
truth
that you
    are common
    and ordinary
    and you fucking
    know it.

BLOOD OF CAESAR

is dust & paper cups
digital photos
Papal lust
beer bottle Pantheons
& hollow-eyed
marble busts,
brothels, & barriers
& barbarian souvenir shops
    selling shreds
    from the bones
    of the empire
    clumps of hair
    & fingernail clippings
gladiators
wearing cheap watches
in cheap costumes
praetorians with prison tattoos
begging for Euros
    to pose
    & pretend
    to be
    noble

      again
      to be
      ghosts
or anything
but lost
to the memory
of   tyrants   who   control   the   chronology.

AT THE FOUNTAIN

holding forum
at the fountain
piazza dei
    whatever
beer, gelato,
macchiato,
    wise words
& discourse
cultural
archeology
    tongues
    trading
    totems
    on society
    history
    politics
    art & war
    on stone
    older than god
Masonic mastery
polished softly
with the melody

of language
between strangers
beautiful intercourse
of nations touching
intimate & delicate
ideas slither & coil
round each other
in soft motions
      curling into
heated bursts
of oral & intellectual
      pleasure.

ROMAN NOON

the perfume
of an elder pine
the distant voice
of a flowery woman
reciting the
wild poetry
of Italian
answering
the phone
      somewhere
in the steep
catacombs
& escarpment
of high rise
luxury apartments
      a gentle wind
birds screech
& sing
a dog barks
tree limbs sway
the sun is high
& bright & so am I

possessed
by the spirit
of ROME
taken back
calm & relaxed
in the safety
of side streets
& anonymity
      far, far away
from the sideshow
of crumbled
& corrupt
kingdoms
of old & new
that parse
the narrative
into retail
spaces
so I sip
from a tiny
chalice
of strong
espresso
fingers

furiously
capturing
every second
every breath
to soak
in this
fragile
moment.

PIAZZA de RENZI

house vino
two bottles
    ½ liter
white
sweet & dry
steaming plate of
gnocchi
    (fresh on Thursdays)
caprese w/tomato
rigatoni (cheese & peppers)
motorbikes
blowing by
straddled
by exotic
women
in Capri pants
    who speak
    w/their hands
flora of accents
me, in my
    Capone hat
seated on

ancient streets
beneath an azure
sky – sun setting
clouds washing by
on the careless
current of the eastern
wind
      baby buildings,
      300 years old
me & she
feathered &
tethered
by a
      flashing spell
of romance &
adventure.

CHEAP WINE

      drunk
on
cheap wine
      collapsed
within
the warm
skin
of each
other
sloppy
lips
wet
kisses
     hot
     hard
     sex
hair tearing
jaw clenching
fists full
of sheet
     don't care
     who hears

speaking
in tongues
muscles
flexed
pulsing
to the
beat
of the
urge
of the
primal
surge
of the
savage
to rip
the veil
to
pieces
to
punch
thru
the membrane
& feast
on the sweet

meat
devouring
salvation
    as we
    cum
    like atoms
    bursting
    into quasars
erupting
into oceans
boiling
radiant
embers
exploding
& coating
the space
between us
    then
    silence
    except
    the rhythm
    of pounding hearts
    of trembled
    breath

a slight
giggle
drifting
into coma
sleep
warm
together
limb
to limb
    no words
soak in
the moment
frantic
& then
beautiful nothing
    two
      bodies
    lay quiet
soft flesh
wet with
love & sweat
against
the silence
of the open

air
and barren
room.

RINGWORM

      s
      h
      e
rots
in the perfect
palace
I have built
for her
    s
    he
    rots
in the cradle
of her
magnetic mind
leaping
like an insect
on fire
room to room
nest
to nest
    life
    is breaking in

        and stabbing
        down
blades
and banes
silence
is the
only
answer
to
the
screaming
questions,
        ok...so?
        what?
        tell me?
        what the fuck now?
        what the fuck do
        you want from me?
        I'm here, aren't I?
taking your shit,
listening to the weakness
dribble down your lips.
I am exhausted
and

hollow, and now
I know
  I don't fucking care
  anymore
  fuck all and fuck off
push me away
once more
and I'll go
forever
  irrevocable
I won't come back
I don't come back
to butchers
hymenical trust
ripped apart
to destroy us
on purpose
  you
   did this
   ringworm
    i r r e v o c a b l e
remember this &
remember these
words

            for-ever
YOU   did   this.

SLOW NIGHT

words
    em tea
    of meaning
wander
the air
like lonely
smoke
primitive
clicks
& coos
circling
the room
barren
of gain
    dreams
going nowhere
fast
serial
planners
serial planning
    someday
we will do

```
        something
        oh yes
                someday
        we will do
        something
        that will
        change the world
        something
        that matters
        something
        that will mean something
        something
                        about Nothing
                someday
        we will show them
        what we're made of
                someday
        we will
        make the perfect film
        sing the perfect song
        write the perfect book
        create the perfect thing
        that no one else
        can even ever imagine
```

   someday
we will get our shit together
   someday
we will get the fuck out of here
   someday
it will all come to us
   someday
we will say
just look at what we've done
   someday
they will regret not believing in us
   someday
soon
but not today
we don't want to rush
into anything
without thinking about it
thoroughly
but someday
oh boy
someday
soon
we will do it all
but not today,

today
we drink
and drink
and think
and speak
about it
conspire and revise
the master plan
over and again
but don't doubt
for what we are about
to do
      someday
will change
everything
      someday
      some way
      we will do it
      carpe ...some day

I mean, just think
what we could do
if we just did it
some day,

some   day   soon.

CONNECTION

a toast
a drink
a handshake
a wink
a secret
a vow
a whisper
a frown
a moment
astounds
a glare
a stare
      her lips
      her hair
      their fists
      locked hips
      against the wall
      on this quiet night
      the lovely
      sound
      fucking
      by candle light

next room
completely unaware
of the triumph
of strangers
sought across
tables
in the dark
dinner party
liaisons
returning to seats
named and marked
a cipher
    of trust
    of lust
    of opening filters
    to receive the light
    to living life
    for all its
    earthly delights
manic doses
of liberation
taken in phases
    to break the chains
    that enslave us

the guru says
my beloved friends
it is prudent
    so   do   it.

MID NIGHT MARE

hooves on the earth
crushing weight
stampeding
in the inky black
hearts
wrapped
in moonlight
heavy breath
twisted mane
eyes wild
enraged
by the serpent
in the fray
fang and scale
a quick
kiss
on the
slobbering
lips
of the young
daughter or son

heavy step
warning
of death
protector &
keeper
just stay away
we are unafraid
stay away stay
away stay away
we are unafraid
stay away stay
away stay away
stay away stay
we are unafraid
away stay away
stay away stay
away stay away
stay   away   stay   away.

RODENT KING

      panic
      when
      the
      alert
      chimes
      in
NEW
MESSAGE
      and I see
        it's from THEM
        on behalf of HIM
and it's a
muddle
of nonsense
accusations
and excuses
      (mostly excuses)
distractions
paragraphs
of fists
pummeling
my psychology

to forget
my self
to lose
my way
to accept
the lies
the excuses
    (mostly excuses)
from their rodent king
and my spirit
rises up
on fire
    and I
    want to
    burn HIS
    fucking
    bloated
    rodent
    world
    to ash
I
want to
destroy
them

for being
stupid
for being
weak
for belonging
to him
for being
eagerly blind
for being
lap dogs
for their
rodent king
starving
mutts
on the cold steps
of entitlement
but
I
inhale
to
take a moment
    to compress
    to let
    the fire

        smolder back
        to the core of me
and
I
summon
my
inner Aurelius
while
cribbing Corleone
and
I
      hide
      the
      rage
      and pain
      and regret
in a simple
      retort
using
big words
with lots of
syllables
      and metaphors
to confuse

and diffuse
their meager
minds
    clandestine
insults
and vulgar
offenses
committed
in self
defense
    against
the slobbering
barbarian hordes
and rotting whores
of the rodent king
    and his greedy
    bloated ego machine
this is a world
where the rats
poison themselves
so to hell
with them
let them gnaw
and steal

on poisonous evils
we are raw
copper plated
titanium & steel
unleash the irons
open the gates
welcome the war
the shell is fractured
can't reverse the atomic reaction
I'm built for the siege
signed and sealed
torch the deal
to the trenches
my brethren
    to
    WIN
    to
    WIN
    to
    WIN.

EX O

paralytic
soul/mind/era
    suffocating
inside
this
hardened
shell
    trapped
on my back
legs
kicking
like an insect
aching
    to move
    to breathe
    to exceed
organs
slipping
through
the stiff
tubes
of limbs

muscles
liquefying
squirming
fat little worm
in tight armor
praying
for
    anything
    other than
    this
    fringe
    borderline
    extremists
    reality
        prefer the
        fantasy
of being wrapped in the grasp of love, mummified forever, moon and tide, enchanted attraction, eyes gripped to slits praying for actuality to manifest, so I keep rolling, side to side, back to front slowing folding over to get back on my front foot so I can race away, race away,   race   away.

WET LUNG

strange gravity
on this empty night
inside
my empty plight
    booze fueled
    solitary
    confinement
    in hale
    ex hale
tee-vee buzzing
about something
    someone said
    someone did
    someone else
something
    about nothing
somewhere else
    not here
    not me
so who cares
    about the wads
    of money

       burning in DC
who cares about
       my barren pockets
       my vacant heart
       my open mind
       my shrinking
       waistline
       unwritten checks
       & desperate acts
       we are pests
to the market
to be exterminated
to be eliminated
from the hue
of the living
bland
not peculiar
the way they
shape the world
crush all resistance
       seek & destroy
the sure cure
for my weighted
agony

                is right there
                across the room
        the key to abate
        these soggy chains
        is 7.2 steps away
        but I can't summon
        even a single
        blast of
        nerve
        cycling energy
        to free me
        from this
                        slow
                        tar
                        pit
                        trap
        to put my feet
        on solid ground
        to whip my arm
        up and around
        my hand
        to grip & grab
        the solution
        the soft revolution

to create
the way
out
so I remain
clicking keys
and fashioning words
as if
this
thing
        somehow
        matters
at all
to anyone
anywhere
    besides me
you see
they've stolen
most of it from
my soul
sick & twisted
stillborn
babies
of Prometheus
silk suits

and designer shoes
jet set
to the Bahamas
and French finger foods
but
    I keep
    trying
    I keep
    typing
    I keep
    writing
    I keep
    fighting
against
the cold
clutching
my soul
hoping
    the words
will warm
me
hoping
    the words
will inflate me

& I can
flee like a
photon
from the
sinister chemists
dehydrating
the wet lung
of   imagination.

THE WHOLE THING

when the pigs move in
and rats and vermin
      think they've got you
remember
      this truth

         life is absurd
so   keep   laughing.

OCCUPY EVERYWHERE

the thrum of the asphalt
alive with grappled breath
tears and sweat
      of a boot-strap nation
      waging holy war
against diamond shined
boot-heel militias
crushing weathered faces
      that crack to smile
      that take & create
      any chance to dance
      that breathe to dream
      to believe
      in something bigger
      than the microcosm
      they've been hemmed in
      to receive
but
hope
is a torch
in the darkness
even a flicker

a sharp spark
can light the way
a single flame
a single ray
can light a million more
so burn until it hurts
until you explode
until there is nothing left for them to exploit and expose.

A BEE

just landed next to me
and my immediate
instinct was
to incite the guards
to ignite the charge
to end this infiltrator
before it attacks me

but it didn't seem hostile
it didn't do anything
except clean its wings
and wipe its eyes
and stumble a bit
when the wind kicked up

so I sat perfectly still
and it allowed me to see
how beautiful
& magnificent
a creature
like this can be

armored
& sculpted
the edges
& contours
fantastically
aerodynamic
silent &
contemplative
cartographer
mapping the landscape
black and gold
little Buddha
light pilot
reciting
little hymns
nibbled along
the edges of its
incredible wings
to remove the
toxins that foster
resistance & stress

and I understood
the reciprocal differences

and what connects

though both
of us are capable
of killing in defense
we refrained
      call it a truce
      between beasts

      I could
have crushed its fuzzy body
      it could
have punctured my lung with a sting

but how could I blame it
for wanting to land here?
it was pleasant
beside me
Muddy Waters
snaking from laptop
speakers
beneath the bright blue
expanse of a hot Los Angeles
December afternoon

me & this bee
taking a moment
to catch our breath
to catch some zen
before resuming our duty
to save the planet
by pollinating every
flower			we			see.

COMPASSIONATE ENTOMOLOGY

a thought
frosted across
my mind
and I was
inclined
to propose
the notion
that if these
things could scream
when we killed them
    would we
    still be
    so eager?

if we heard
the pain they felt
would we?
could we?

break them
to pieces?
would sound

make them
invincible
to   our   rash   sensibilities?

HATS & BATS

badges & body armor
zip ties & flash grenades
chemical weapons & non-lethal
crowd control technologies
uniformed & razor jawed
painted thugs for the autocracy
    holding the line
    toe to nose
    with the wide eyes of
    love & courage
    passive
    peaceful
    non-violent people
    devoted to
    civil disobedience
Power of the People
Power to the People
    We, The People
    unblinking
    unwavering
even as the threats are hurled
    & the batons are raised

    && all hell breaks loose
    in a violent rain
    of rubber bullets
    & flash grenades
    they remain
stoic in the storm
they sit their ground
a human chain
    elbows linked
    scared but brave
    enough to stay
    unarmed
    & take the blows
to be battered by the finest
paramilitary force in the world
    blood
    is in the water
    and on our faces
we are hungry
and they are full
but fools can't enter heaven
with empty hearts
and swollen pockets
    and brother, that's the gospel

so as
the riot police
line up in force
the free people
    stay strong
    calm & devoted
to bring peace to a land of War
to speak as one
of many
in a single voice

    WE ARE UNSTOPPABLE
    ANOTHER WORLD IS POSSIBLE

we   are   you   and   we   are   one.

WIDOW AT THE WINDOW

walking
this life
through

      new corridors
      and estuaries
      lush gardens
      and crystal seas

the plush rugs
made of pearl
and blood
pollinated
by the sex magick
of poetry

          for a moment
          my eyes
          peek
          between
          our
          narrow

worlds
and
I reflect on things
that might have been

the many
phases
of infection
I escaped
in the past
tense

a lifeless sack
of skin and bone
hanging from
the rafters
like a
dishrag
on a hook
wet
& heavy

a coiled
ivory
slug
anchored
at the
bottom
of the
murky tub
ribbons
of crimson
rising like
atomic war

or

        a huddled mass
        weeping into
        fists full of
        twisted blankets
        wondering
        why I am still here
        why I take this shit
        why I allow others
        to dictate my happiness

a widow
at the window

staring out
at a life
that died

and then I exhale
and a smile
paints itself
across my skull
      what is
is all
      that matters

I endured
I survived
it took time
to become
King of the Lesbians
heavy crown
happy home
art in my blood

poetry on my breath
architect of my own
kingdom
and sea
every nail
every hammer forged
was born
from my
supernatural
stubborn abilities
    I do
    whatever I have
    to do
I click keys for a living
at 3AM in an empty room

ignoring the warm body
skin like moonlight
dreaming heavy
patient at rest
beside me
    because I can't slow down
    because the moment is here now
    because this

is immortal
and she isn't.

MISS

excuse me,
yes, hello, dawn breaker,
    eyes soft
    and wet
    with the wild world,
I think I'll have
something
more   to   dream.

CAVITY

this hole
open
and cold
    size of a fist
    cauterized
    along the
    leathered edges
striking frozen
bone
& artery
cracked
like glass
this mask
I see
of me
I don't recognize
the eyes staring
into the fragmented
ashes of my charcoaled heart
    a heart that split
    a heart that aches
    a happy heart

   is the one that breaks
so I trudge forth
carrying the weight
through these
empty rooms
of mausoleum luxury
my home
barren and unknown
to me
   nothing special
   nothing unique
no secrets or smiles to share
the clock ticks without joyful alarm
   it's gone
   our stolen moments
memories heavy and still
like dust on the cupboard
great gravity
   so I seek to soak the walls
   in lust and grateful cries
   from as many women
   as my heart desires
   to dye the stains
   left by your lies

      and duplicity
      with the wet paint
      of soul screaming ecstasy
      to pry any sign of you
      from these rooms
      with bite marks and
      raw, savage fucks
      with tight bodied
      strangers in urgent
      surges of lust
bury my face
inside the delicate
petals
and bellow
      FUCK YOUUUU
      as I explode into her
      body and she into mine
and she giggles a little
and softly asks why and I kiss her
and say, "nothing babe, never mind"
      and she pulls my hair
      and pushes me down
and I feed again
and she screams

in foreign vowels
> hours and hours
> of erasing you
> of negating you
> of sharing breath

with some
. first timer
. gay for a day
. gold-star stranger
. friend with benefits
> someone
> anyone
> more worthy

of me
of this
of everything
than   you   ever   fucking   will   be.

CHARLATAN

when your soul
rose up to mine
to speak the secrets
only I would know
    and we drifted
    across continents
    like vapor
    rolling over
    and in
    to each other
    and we found
    infinity in a
    drop of rain
    in a shaft of
    light streaming
    in from the window shade
and I was under your spell
two souls whispering while
we slept
one listening, the other wept
    as the lie unraveled
    and the rot revealed

   conspiracies and tragedy
   knotted to deceive
you were counterfeit
and I complicit
for cloaking myself
in the fantasy
of what I wanted
not what was there
   for you saw
   the flower in me
   hungry for light
   so the darkness
   in you reflected
   my shine
   and your soul
   pretended to know
   what was written all
   over mine
and
all you had to do
was ask for a clue
when you didn't understand
and my sightless love
was at your command

just ask
>	how to spell a word
>	& pretend
>	to have a broken wing
>	to be the wounded bird
>	and I would come running
>	breathlessly
>	with the sure cure in hand

for a phantom
for a phony
for a forgery
>	of imaginative fiction
>	for shit-filled perfection
>	wrapped in soft eyes
>	and innocence
>	one hand in mine
>	the other in my pocket
>	oh, whatever this is
>	I don't fucking want it

now
through this
house I wander
& when I think of you
I don't know which face to see

which identity to believe
        so I spend my time
        unrolling twine
        cutting cables
        and unraveling knots
        of the sticky
        tangled webs
that the
lanky
spider left
clotting   my   thoughts.

PUSSY

this word,
meant to feminize
and victimize
someone
that is
    weak,
    cowardly,
    frail,
    flimsy,
    timid,
    or meek
is a misnomer
    truth be told
    pussies
are one of the
most durable
organs on the human body
it is rugged and pliable
and believe me, brother,
    I would know,
    I am an expert
so if you are looking

to designate someone as

    weak or delicate

    to label them

    fragile, fearful, or irrelevant

then let's get to the hard heart of the matter – you must, as a responsible antagonist, refer to them as a testicle or a scrotum or something much truer to the nature of the offensive prattle – the wind blows past your laps and brutes crumble to ash – I rest my case – so the next time you want to dare someone to do something dangerous and they back out, don't fumble about with silly absurdities such as, "don't be a pussy" – be righteous in your slight – let them know you have a mastery of the language – unleash your tongue with a lashing that's sure to sting – give them zip with a zing – go for the throat of the coward – "scrotum, smegma" show your power! break the back of the excuse and roar with righteousness something similar or related to   "don't be a testicle, dude".

BLOODSUCKER

there were nights
when you broke
the silence
with a shriek
    'a giant spider
    in the room'
strange the
way they
were always
so called to you
    but now I know
    you were one
    of their own
web weaving
prey deceiving
bloodsucker.

LOOK

at your life
      is it yours?
      does it belong to you?
      or someone else?
your greatest gift
L IF E
      is it between
      your fists
      gripped
      like a sledgehammer?
      are you wearing a disguise?
      to please them
      to fit in
      to not draw attention?
look around you
      are these your people?
      is this who you want to be?
      is this your destiny?
to nuzzle in & bunker down
      to become just like them?
      another nobody who surrendered?
are you pretending?

       are you only there because you're afraid to
be alone?
       are you afraid to make a mistake?
I know
       you feel safe here
       with them
       but you're so sad
              well,
don't you want to be happy?
what are you waiting for?

       stop living
          for someone else.
       stop ignoring
          your destiny
       stop expecting
          something to happen
       stop waiting
          for the moment to arrive
       stop resisting
       start creating
and   just   be   you.

ABOVE ALL

nourishing
my mind
    through
    the eyes
watching
a film
taken
from the
international
space station
orbiting earth
    the phantoms
    of the aurora
    shifting
    weather patterns
    the sparkle of cities
how small
how significantly
insignificant
we must seem
to infinity
    if there is a watcher

   a God or Goddess
   it is no wonder
they ignore our insect wars
and tiny pleas for wealth and power
they are tending
to this beautiful planet
   and our
    snug place
   in space
surrounded
by the ever-expanding
        universe
why should they care
for our pettiness?
   do we bother when colonies
   of ants wage war?
   do we care when the fox
   snaps up a field mouse?
   do we get upset
   when we
   cut down
   a tree
   and a raven
   loses its home?

with debt on our mind?
with the children coughing and sick?
with hunger creeping in our bellies?
with leaked nuclear secrets?
with a sky like today?
with an uprising three states away?
with the blather on the news?
with a moment like this?
with the stereo blasting?
with the windows down?
with the girl of my dreams?
with her head in my lap?
with so much to do?
with nowhere to go?
do we care?
        NO.
no   we   don't.

ON THE WALL

vote out
the politicians
that sold out

finance kings
& botox queens
broken dreams
& broken reality

money ~~can't~~ fixes everything.

TO BEGIN

♡   yourself   1st

FLAME THROWER

I exist on a
meager edge,
a slight acute angle
to their
straight society

I am a bonfire
charcoaling
the
heavy drapes
of darkness
drifting down
from endless
space

I burn
and surge
flames lick
and flicker
to destroy
to reverse
the humdrum

monopoly of monotony
they create

so while the amoebas
maneuver to find their shape
I am busy cobbling a world
too   fragile   to   break.

FOR LOVE

I have been
used up
& beaten down
disregarded
& detained
ripped to pieces
& sewn back into place
    carried the load
      & asked for more
    held my tongue
      when I should've roared
worn many faces
to become an interpretation
    of love
    of loyalty
inside & behind
their sadistic eyes
they see
in me
what they want to see
    molded & shaped
    erased & replaced

I eagerly agreed
  because I thought it would help
  because I thought it would change
the trajectory
flying or falling
it's all the same
when you don't control the rudder
when you are blind at the wheel
when you let another steer

so tell me again
how I am to blame
how it will never be the same
tell me again
how much you love me
how I am the only one
tell me again
how sorry you are
  that you aren't as strong as I am
  that you didn't mean it
  that you aren't perfect
  and neither am I
tell me again
how you know I'm cheating

how this is just the universe speaking
that pretext is justified as long as it benefits you
that this pain is felt by both
that you know
and I know
it's the right thing
      and I watch
      and I listen
as the fat serpents of deception
vomit from the red slits
of your paper cut lips
falling heavy to the floor
slithering over
and coiling
around my limbs
to draw me back in
to become the strings
for I, your puppet
to dance and sing
to protect and provide
everything
you need
      but not this time
      I've become frozen

        a wedge of malice
        has knifed inside
        my shattered heart
        and I no longer know you
        or recognize the language you speak
my spirit leaves before I do
closing the door
my hand
switches
the lock behind you
mites do not trouble me
I search my soul
and there's no love left
for the fiction of us
for the grand lie
we lived
orchestrated by you
and your grifter heart
and I find inside the
loneliness, a warmth
a belief, a determination
to cut away the anchors
to abate this drape of shade
that has hidden the light

from my eyes
for too long
now I see through the haze
    somewhere
the sun is shining
    somewhere
the sky is as blue
as a robin's egg
    and laughter
    and love
    and beauty
float like feathers
on the gentle air
I know it's there
    somewhere
and I'm leaving
all of this
and you
well behind
to   find   it.

BIG RED

she passed
into past
on a day
like today
    bright sky
    low heat
    quaint &
    unremarkable
prior to exodus
she was whipping
the sun chariot
at blazing speeds
satellites & jetpacks
    before her time
    ahead of the pack
conquering 50 foot
swells to Catalina
blustering squalls
factory riveting
in the Great War
picking cotton
& berries

in the summer sun
trips to Spain & back
on ocean liners &
piloting aircraft
out of Long Beach
on Cherry Street
  fireball
  lung lifter
  the rock
we were
happy
in her gravity
like the singing moons
of Jupiter
and then
just like that
she evaporated
  94 years
  for us
  gone in a flash
her fire ghosted to smoke
hollow
leaving a husk
of the pioneer

she was
like a rocket
that ran out of fuel
& landed softly
in a field of posies
quiet wreckage
  dents & cracks in the paint
  fractured left axle
  aft thrusters &
  guidance systems
  misfiring but intact
but, oh, the atmospheres she climbed
the private serenities she'd seen
the magic & mysteries
kingdoms of cloud & exotic seas
  a noble life, a chieftain,
  always needed
letters from Africa
casinos across the continents
card games & Victrolas
yacht clubs & bread lines
  rising up
  from the
  Great Depression

      cobbling a life
      from the lumber
      of strife
pouring from the bottle
what she had into her loved ones
      we wept in awe
      for what we saw
           a trajectory that was high & long
she didn't crash & burn
           she steered through the weather
           she soared high against the sun
           & spread a long shadow
over the earth
that   will   burn   within   us   forever.

ONE TRUTH

the one truth
no artist can escape
whether writer, poet,
painter, sculptor, et cetera, et al
is that
    we require experience
    we require data
    we need to soak in life
even when the anchors of reality
pull us beneath the blankets
even when we feel
we must drown
our minds
in hard drink & chemicals
    we need to be
    out there
feeding
from the
vein
of existence.

SPIRITUAL INTERCOURSE

there are moments
when I brave the stage
    gladiator
      in the arena

and the lights are dimmed
and the air is tense
and the audience have summoned
a landmine atmosphere
one more step

      & everything will explode

but I maneuver delicately
to keep the tension thick
to tickle their spirits
    with anticipation

and at this moment
when all breath is hushed
when all eyes are locked

I can taste their souls
raw and hot
passing through me

and this is the moment
      of spiritual intercourse

when gender, race, gay or straight,
fiscal backgrounds, political affiliations,
or lack thereof, cease to exist

the only component
in this trembling moment
is that we are all here
surrendering to an
      orgy of the
collective subconscious
entering bliss
& forfeiting ego
walls crumble & away we go
      vulnerability
      rockets us into strange
atmospheres
      to sparkle among the stars to form

       our own constellation
and then when the brilliance is just right
when we twinkle like diamonds
from the shine of our own light
       I plant my foot
back on the soil
& everything erupts
and voices boil
back to the point
our souls
just climbed
and bodies shiver
& collide
       & who we are outside
those doors ceases to matter
we discard the cloak
we abate the disguise

we embrace our savage souls
as gods, messiahs, prophets,
saviors, soldiers, lovers, leaders,
dreamers, artists, activists, and believers

the music spirals

the ritual ends
      and we leave our world
for it to return
to a beer soaked tavern
      but the lessons we learned
are burned
into the retinas of our soul
      it will always be there
shaping the way
our   hearts   guide   us   home.

NOTICE TO THE HUMAN RACE

it was Florida
outside
some bar
some drunk asshole
    almost
ran over my dogs
he backed out without looking
and drove over the curb
    almost
crushing us
as we walked
on the grassy path

lucky for him
I only
    almost
    murdered him
lucky for him
    I have predator instincts
and pulled them to safety
in the nick of time
and when I roared in protest

       he drove away in fear,
          otherwise,
I would have gouged out his eyes, bit off his nose, and kicked him in the scrotum until I broke his pelvic bone, then I would have disgorged his heart with my thumb and jaw and shoved it down his choking throat and set his struggling body on fire.

        NOTICE TO THE HUMAN RAT RACE.

no   one   fucks   with   my   dogs.

FEMININE FORCE

I am amazing
and they know it

I'm a strong woman
physically, mentally, spiritually

I'm a strong human
physically, mentally, spiritually

the weaker sheeple will do their best to shackle
me within their black & gray society

        but it won't change a thing

I'm a strong woman
physically, mentally, spiritually

I'm a strong human
physically, mentally, spiritually

I can do what they can do
(and sometimes better)
but can they follow suit?

hardly ever

I can

    out-think them
    out-fight them
    out fuck them

I can create macrocosms that their meager imaginations will never fully grasp or be able to understand

    I am amazing
    and they know it

    I am amazing
    and they fear me for it

this is why they place the chains on me
this is why they place the blame on me

when the mere mention of me arises
their egos shrivel like a scrotum in ice water

they hate me, cuz they ain't me

      because I'm capable
      because I'm unbreakable
      because I'm unafraid

as an artist, I'm unstoppable
as a thinker, I'm incomparable
as a lover, well brother, you can
      outlaw my sexuality,
      my equal rights,
      but it will never change
      the fact that
      I get more pussy
      than you do
but I digress

keep lobbing those molotovs of hatred & bigotry
   - I'm fireproof

keep firing your rifles of ego,
   - I'm bulletproof

the more pressure you apply
the freer I become
because I love myself
      first

unconditionally
I am perfectly unique
I live to defy

I   AM   I

DEF POETRY

    [notes
    on def]
fourth of February
2004
    arrived
busy hotel
after bouncy flight
    times square
met the producers on the set
stage craft
architecture
    Stan Latham/producer
a swell gentlemen
sat in the seats
took in the rules
showed our clothes
to the camera / no white shirts / no slogans
    then the line up
walk & words
into the eye
of the camera
    my time

       arrived
raw rehearsal,
I fucked up
I recovered well
       – no one else knew – but me.

I sat in my hotel room petrified
hysterical, sometimes crying
so ashamed & angry at myself
for almost blowing this chance
this moment, to be enchanted
to be enchanting, I read the words
over and over and over and over
desperate to etch them into my memory
is this what I wanted? to come all this way just to fail and bury a thorn of regret inside my mind for the rest of my rugged life? no. I would sustain.

       I would be ready
when my moment came
       I pushed
       all the panic & terror
       into the furnace
       of my desires

       and I burned it all
       as fuel for the performance

this was my first time
to ever do anything like this
my first time
to ever perform my poetry
to anyone
other than my reflection
on lonely nights in western Los Angeles

       and I did it
       on fucking HBO

the poem was titled
Dedicated to my Enemy

       at 1st
my words began like a foreign language
that I could pronounce but not understand

       flowery vowels and doughy consonants
       and strange clicking sounds but soon –
       the frequency soaked in – and I found my
       wave and it broke and raised to tsunami

        and I remember thinking

the stage was low
and the lights bright
and the audience was mine
        tonight
I stepped out
with no one to rely on
with no one to answer for failure
        but me
and
I did it

the audience was
breathless and joyful
and perhaps a little afraid
still
I was told
I was the antidote
to the pre-fabricated
mode
of poetic performance

I was "on fire up there"

I was "very brave"

I had "conquered the show"

but it didn't matter, truly, because I was proud of me.

I spent a sleepless night in New York City

smiling / I met Russell Simmons, a real gentleman / I met Mos Def, a real artist

    I went back to my hotel with a poet I met after the show

        she and I rewrote the Odyssey

        on soft cotton sheets and created our own language that only we could speak

I spent a sleepless night in N Y C, smiling

like a flower without the

thorns   of   regret.

LOVING HOME

you're ugly and inadequate
stupid and a slave in a wasted life
a dreamer, a loser, worthless, irresponsible
predictable, and preposterous,

> you should'a never been born
> you pathetic abnormal
> gifted child
>
> that could draw before
> she could talk

not enough
too much

> too short
> too fat
> too skinny
> ungrateful
> idiotic
> deep voiced
> ingrate

too many freckles
too blonde
too angry
too different
too much like me
too tom-boyish
too simple
too complex

    on and on
    more and more
    again and again

    well fuck them
    I survived my life
    and so you can

dear
fat girl
gay boy
black kid
immigrant
slant-eyed
thick lipped

big hipped
citizen

of the State of Hypocrisy we were never meant to
be anything, nothing but a nest of enemies
but if we tried
to unify
our strength
into love
the power
could shift
the pillars
of the world

if we
could stop
pretending
that what
they thought
mattered
well .....

      it doesn't
      so   now   what?

FOUNDER OF THE FEAST

a hungry child
on the steps outside
but the church stays closed
no glimpse of Christ

just the jewels of a priest
polished and cleaned
by a child
who has no money to buy
his ticket to ride
inside the belly of the Wish God
who's   deaf   &   blind.

SOMEBODY PLEASE

just fucking listen to us
you don't have to have an answer
we just need to discuss
    how things got fucked
    how things got tough
    how we just want to erupt
and when we have no one to turn to
at least we have you
and the beautiful courage
of your concrete
silence so
please
just
be
there
for me
please
just   listen.

GRAVE WORDS

they say
to be remembered
you must put the
ART in mARTyr

to suck it up
says Sylvia

take it in
raves Cobain

or hide in my
miracles like Howard
or sell my soul
for Faustian powers

just to be complete
just to be another

Moses
Lennon
Morrison

Tupac
Joan of Arc
Gandhi
Rosa Parks
Marquis de Sade
Ginsberg
Kerouac
Langston
Plath

but this will not be
even when the world is heavy
it's still pretty swell to be me

    so I will
    ignite the
    fuel
    a little
    spark
    destroying
    the dark

another
lover

who wants
to save
butchered
lambs
from
future
scams
and hope
to provoke
nightly
good
great
goddamns

villains will use wide brushes
and the stories always get painted
with just enough hue
to distort the truth

so let me write
a psalm or two
for you
that inks the night
into the oceans of

your eyes
on your skin with my lips
and hide inside
the energy of our smiles.

ITHACA

you can believe
all those things
you try to deceive
me
with
but I know
you were never
my Ithaca
you were simply
the broken boat
I mistakenly chose
to get me there

so I will swim
until I grow fins
or until I see
the glorious shore welcoming me.

DON'T GO

there are times when some of us feel as if our lives have no meaning yet our hearts surge with a hunger for substance and significance. this means something. it means you feel more than others, it means your soul understands before your brain does.

in this age, in this era, you must know how rare this gift is. and if you don't, I do. so, if you are ever seriously considering committing suicide, I would ask (as a personal favor) that you don't.

there aren't many who can see the world the way you do. bullies and cronies destroy themselves. in time, they cannibalize. so stop allowing them to inhabit you.

it is important that you understand the only thing you can rely on is change. you cannot go, you must remain. all of this will soon go away. so stay. I would dare say you are duty bound to do so because some will never know the depth of emotion that you experience.

So Glow.
Burn.
IGNITE.

but do not remove your hue from this bland world, DETONATE IT!

be brave,
be bold,
BURN BRIGHT!

       Life is short, but life goes on.
so take your chance! the chance you deserve.
live the life you want. create it! RADIATE IT!
          make it so!

end.

thank you for letting me inside
your eyes.

sadistic
scribbles

Burning soul into charcoal and sketching dreams into reality ....

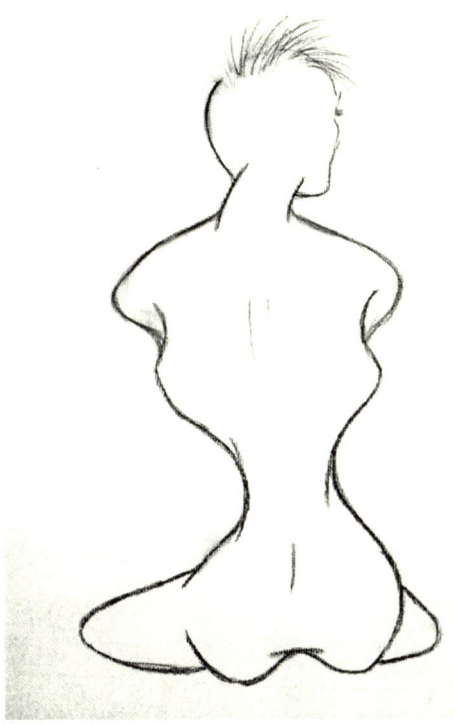

Otep Shamaya is an artist, activist, author, a 2010 GLAAD nominee, cultural arsonist, & intellectual loudmouth with a fearless passion for justice & the preservation of the arts.

Live to Defy.

This is her second collection of printed poetry.

NEW WORD ORDER
The Poetry Of Otep Shamaya

Centaurs Breed Publishing

For information about this publication contact:
you@artsaves.me or online at www.otepsaves.me

Cover design & additional illustrative contribution
by Joey James www.joeyjamesart.com

All words & images copyright © OTEP SHAMAYA 2011
All Rights Reserved.